Country Tea Parties

Maggie Stuckey
Illustrations by Carolyn Bucha

A Storey Publishing Book

STOREY

Storey Communications, Inc.
Schoolhouse Road
Pownal, Vermont 05261

The mission of Storey Communications is to serve our customers by publishing practical information that encourages personal independence in harmony with the environment.

Edited by Gwen W. Steege
Design and production by Cynthia N. McFarland

Printed in Mexico

10 9 8 7 6 5 4 3 2 1

Library of Congress Cataloging-in-Publication Data

Stuckey, Maggie.
    Country Tea Parties / Maggie Stuckey ; illustrations by Carolyn Bucha.
        p.   cm.
    Includes index.
    ISBN 0-88266-935-4 (hc : alk paper)
        1. Afternoon teas—United States. 2. Tea—United States.
3. Confectionary—United States. I. Title.
    TX736.S78 1996
    641.5'3—dc20
                                                96-2005
                                                CIP

Contents

I. THE TEAS

*O*f the more than 3,000 varieties of tea (not including herb teas), all begin with the dried leaves of one plant: *Camellia sinensis*. This species of *Camellia* grows throughout Asia, and develops slightly different tastes depending upon the soil, climate, and elevation. When harvested, dried, and processed, these leaves become what is collectively known as black tea. Tea names often indicate geographic origin: Assam is a province in northern India, Ceylon tea comes from Sri Lanka, and Darjeeling is a district in the foothills of the Himalayas.

Most packaged tea is a blend of two or more varieties: English Breakfast and Irish Breakfast, for instance, as well as just-plain-tea in teabags. Scented teas are flavored with essential oils of flowers, fruits, and spices. The most popular is Earl Grey, which contains orange oil. Orange pekoe, incidentally, is not a variety or a blend but a term that designates size of the tea leaf.

Tea leaves release their flavor in water — the hotter the water, the faster the tea steeps. Brewing with boiling water takes 5 minutes, sun tea can take an hour, and refrigerator tea takes several hours.

In ancient times tea leaves compressed into embossed bricks were used for money.

Herb Tea

Herb teas are lighter in color than brewed black tea; judge readiness by fragrance and taste, not color.

Herbal tea is made by steeping the leaves, stems, flowers, or roots of that large group of flavorful plants known as herbs. Some of these plants have documented medicinal properties, and herb teas have a long tradition as healing drinks. Herb teas also contain no caffeine, contributing to their healthful reputation. But if you think of herb tea only for its medicinal value you are missing a lot of tea pleasure. Whereas all types of black tea fall on one taste spectrum, herb teas give us a full rainbow of flavors.

Commercial manufacturers have developed many delicious and winsomely named concoctions: wholly herbal combinations as well as blends of herb and black teas. (If the package says "caffeine-free," it's an all-herbal blend.)

If you grow herbs in your garden, you can have the fun of making your own tea blends. But even if you don't, you can experiment by adding commercial herb products like anise, fennel, and caraway seed to regular tea.

When using a screw-together tea ball, fill it only halfway; loose tea expands severalfold when it steeps.

How to Make a Perfect Pot of Tea

Start with cold water, and bring it to a boil. Meanwhile, prewarm your teapot by filling it with hot water from the tap. As soon as the water boils, empty the teapot and measure in your tea: approximately 1 teaspoon for each cup of tea. (Why do you think it's called a *tea*spoon?) Tradition demands that you bring the teapot to the kettle and pour in the boiling water. Let steep for 3 to 5 minutes. The exact timing depends on your taste preferences and on the tea you start with: large leaves take longer.

Using a tea ball to hold the loose tea makes things much simpler; you won't have to strain the tea into the cups, and you can remove it so the tea doesn't get too strong.

Are Teabags Legitimate?

Teabags were accidentally invented in 1904 by a New York tea merchant named William Sullivan, who hit upon the idea of sending samples to customers in hand-sewn silk bags, rather than the more common tea tins. He was soon flooded with orders — for tea in the convenient little bags.

Many tea aficionados — British and American alike — disdain teabags as inferior at best and sacrilegious at worst. The tea particles in bags are smaller and thus brew more quickly; if you leave a bag to brew as long as you would loose tea, you'll get something akin to battery acid. Used properly, however, teabags make an acceptable cup of tea. In my view, wasting food is a sacrilege; teabags are a common-sense convenience. How the taste compares is one of the great questions of life you must decide for yourself.

Spiced Tea

Store sugar cubes for tea in a jar with whole cloves or cinnamon sticks. They will absorb the spicy fragrance.

Experiment with the many wonderful blends offered by commercial tea companies and then, next time you're in the supermarket, scoot over to the spice aisle and the produce section and buy the ingredients to make your own spiced tea.

From the spice section: whole cinnamon, cloves, allspice, and nutmeg. Don't use powdered spices; they leave a gritty residue. The process is simplicity itself: put a small amount of spices (one or a combination) in the teakettle; by the time the water boils, some of their flavor is extracted.

From the produce section, get a chunk of fresh ginger root. Slice it crosswise into pieces about ¼ inch thick (peeling not necessary), and whack them with the flat side of your knife to release the flavor. Simmer a few slices in the tea water. If you can't find fresh ginger, crystallized ginger works too. Strain off the spices and serve in your prettiest cups.

Iced Tea

In 1904, the World's Fair was held in St. Louis. To promote tea drinking among Americans, a conglomerate of British tea merchants sponsored a booth offering free samples. But it was hot in St. Louis that summer, and fair visitors were having none of it. Finally, the exhibition director, an Englishman named Blechynden, himself sweltering, poured the hot tea into glasses filled with ice — and invented a new drink.

Three Ways to Make Iced Tea

❖ **Brewed tea:** Make tea approximately double strength and steep only five minutes. Pour into a pitcher, over an equal amount of ice. (If your pitcher is glass, let the tea cool before pouring it in.) If you sweeten the tea while it is hot, you'll need only half as much sugar.

❖ **Sun tea:** Place 1 teaspoon loose tea or one teabag per pint tap water (with sugar, if you wish) in a glass jar or pitcher. Cover and set in the sun for an hour or so. Timing is not critical — because the water doesn't boil, the tea will not get bitter.

❖ **Refrigerator tea:** Follow procedure for sun tea, except brew in refrigerator overnight. Two advantages: when it's done, it's already cold; and no matter how long it sits, it doesn't get cloudy.

For iced tea, make special ice cubes that won't dilute the tea: fill ice trays with tea, apple juice, berry juice, lemonade, mint water, or ginger water and freeze.

❖

Fruit-flavored and spiced teas from commercial manufacturers make delicious iced tea.

❖

Mix 1 jigger of brandy with 2 cups tea; freeze in ice cube tray. Use for iced tea at a late-afternoon party.

❖

Stash iced-tea glasses in the freezer an hour before the party.

II. THE TEA PARTIES

$\mathcal{G}$iving tea parties is an old idea that seems new again. The soothing atmosphere that inevitably accompanies a pot of tea is especially welcome in an increasingly frenetic world, and sharing that feeling is a wonderful way to entertain.

In the twelve parties ahead, you will find many traditional British tea treats (some of them Americanized) along with familiar American foods adapted for tea parties. Recipes for very common items are not included because I know you can find them in the cookbooks on your shelves. (Note: an asterisk* appears on the menus next to recipes that are included here.) Instead, you will find menu suggestions and abbreviated instructions, which I hope you will think of as raw material for your own creativity.

This is intended to be an idea book, and it presumes a mix-and-match approach: take any item from any month and use it anywhere else. For example, the tart pastry technique described for June's Maids of Honor can be used to make miniature pecan pies in December. Make May's Pastry Puffs and fill them with salmon mousse in January. Take the Honey-Orange Butter from March and convert it to raspberry butter for July. Read about puff pastry in December, and use it to make chicken salad turnovers in May. You'll think of dozens of other creative ideas as you plan your own parties.

For large parties, prepare a strong tea concentrate ahead of time: Use 4 teabags per 1 cup of boiling water; steep 2 minutes, then strain; leave at room temperature. During the party keep a large kettle of water simmering on the stove. For each serving, add ½ cup hot water to ⅛ cup concentrate.

Tea Classics

The British, who invented the late afternoon meal called *tea,* are also responsible for the classic tea-time treats that sometimes mystify Americans.

Crumpets are griddle cakes that develop surface holes as they cook, the better to catch melting butter. Acceptable substitute: English muffins from the supermarket.

Scones are essentially light, tender biscuits, served hot from the oven with jam and butter or clotted cream. A basic recipe is on page 48; variations are unlimited. You can add raisins, dried currants, nuts, orange or lemon zest, berries, banana, cheese, herbs, spices, molasses, even chocolate chips. Some very nice commercial mixes are available on the supermarket shelves next to the biscuit mix (and in a pinch, you can even use *that* — just don't tell).

Lemon curd is a thick sauce, about the consistency of pudding, that is spread on crumpets and muffins like jam, and used as a filling for tarts. You can purchase it in gourmet food shops or in the jelly section of some large supermarkets, or use the recipe on page 45.

Clotted cream, also called *Devon cream,* is made in Devonshire, England, by separating the cream from unhomogenized milk and scalding it until it is extra-thick. True Devon cream is unavailable in the United States, but an acceptable substitute is unsweetened whipped cream.

A Creamy Affair

The very British affair called a *cream tea* is afternoon tea featuring scones and clotted cream (for the scones, not the tea).

Making Tea Sandwiches

You will find a wide assortment of ideas for tea sandwiches scattered throughout this book. For each of them, start with dense, high-quality, bread, — white, whole wheat, rye, and pumpernickel all work well. If you're serving several kinds of sandwiches, use different breads for an attractive presentation. The best bread for tea sandwiches is thinly sliced. Bakeries can often slice whole loaves thinly. In the supermarket, so-called diet bread is often thin-sliced; so are the smaller loaves meant for party canapes.

Then, except where the filling is itself a type of butter, spread the bread very thinly with softened butter. If you make the sandwiches ahead, this keeps the filling from making the bread soggy.

Assemble the sandwiches, refrigerate (cold bread cuts more cleanly), and then, shortly before serving, trim off crusts and cut sandwiches into smaller pieces. You can make fingers (two parallel cuts), triangles (two diagonal cuts), squares (two perpendicular cuts), rounds (with cookie cutter), and any fancy shape you have cutters for. For open-face sandwiches, it's easier to butter, trim, and cut the bread into smaller pieces first, and then place the topping.

Arrange the finished sandwiches on your serving tray and cover with waxed paper and a damp dishtowel until party time.

Afternoon tea was invented by the Duchess of Bedford in the mid 1800s. To tide herself over for a very late dinner, she asked her maid to serve small sandwiches and cakes with her afternoon tea, and a new fashion was born.

$\mathcal{J}$anuary 6, the twelfth day after Christmas, was, in Elizabethan England, the last day of the gala winter holiday season, which may explain why William Shakespeare chose it as the name of one of his most boisterous comedies.

To conclude your own holiday season with a memorable event, host a "Twelfth Night" party. Tell your guests they're invited to a play reading, then collect as many copies of Shakespeare's play from the library as you can. Put the name of the fourteen characters on slips of paper, and ask each guest to draw one. (If you have fewer than fourteen guests, one person can take two minor roles.) For those rusty on their Shakespeare, give a short summary of the plot, and then let the play begin.

When guests first arrive, offer tea, sherry, and a few nibble foods. Serve the buffet supper at the end of Act III, traditional intermission time.

Of course, you could have a plain Twelfth Night party, without the Shakespeare; but I promise you it isn't nearly as much fun.

Herb Scones *
Cheeses and Cold Meats
Spiced Pears *
Devils on Horseback *
Stuffed Mushrooms
Cheese Puff Surprises *
Raspberry Trifle *
Bishop *

Herb Scones

To the Basic Scones recipe (page 48), add about 3 tablespoons of fresh (or 1 tablespoon dried) herbs (basil, thyme, oregano). Serve with softened butter mixed with chopped herbs and a dash of lemon juice.

Spiced Pears

Peel, core, and halve 7 large pears. Combine 1 cup of apple juice with ½ cup sugar, ½ cup fruit vinegar, and whole spices: 2 teaspoons cloves, 1 or 2 cinnamon sticks, 1 teaspoon peppercorns, and 3 bay leaves. Simmer until the sugar is dissolved; add pears, turn off heat, and let them cool in the liquid. Drain well before serving.
SERVES 14

Devils on Horseback

Stuff whole pitted prunes with about 1 teaspoon each of a chutney/cheese mixture (1 part fruit chutney to 2 parts grated sharp cheddar). Wrap half a strip of bacon around each prune; fasten with toothpick. Bake at 400°F until bacon is crisp, about 10 minutes; drain on paper towels.

Cheese Puff Surprises

Drain a 7-ounce jar of stuffed green olives. Make a cheese dough by creaming together 8 ounces grated cheddar, ½ cup butter, 1 cup flour, 1 teaspoon cayenne, and 1 teaspoon paprika. Pinch off small pieces of dough and shape into 1-inch balls; use your thumb to press a crater into the ball. Place an olive into each crater and work the dough over so it is completely covered. Place balls on ungreased cookie sheet and bake for 10–12 minutes at 375°F. The olive balls can be made ahead and frozen; slip straight into the oven unthawed and bake for 15 minutes.
MAKES ABOUT 50 PIECES

Raspberry Trifle

You will need yellow or white cake layers (or those slender cake-like cookies called *ladyfingers*); brandy, fruit liqueur, or fruit juices; apricot preserves or fruit puree (baby food works well); fresh or frozen raspberries; vanilla or lemon pudding; and whipped cream. Served in a clear glass bowl — a classic straight-sided, pedestal trifle dish, if you have one — this traditional layered British dessert makes an elegant centerpiece.

Place a layer of cake on the bottom of the bowl, breaking the cake into pieces to cover the bottom neatly, if necessary. Drizzle on a bit of brandy, fruit liqueur, or fruit juice. Now spread on a thin layer of preserves or pureed fruit, and add half of the raspberries. Top the fruit with the pudding. Place another layer of cake and then the remaining berries, and top with whipped cream. Refrigerate until party time.

Bishop

This hot wine punch is a very, very old British recipe; Jonathan Swift, writing in the eighteenth century, mentions it fondly.

Stick whole cloves into the skin of 4 or 5 oranges, using about 1 tablespoon for each orange. Roast the oranges for ½ hour at 350°F, until they become very fragrant. Meanwhile, simmer 2 cinnamon sticks, 2 tablespoons whole allspice, and 3 round slices of fresh ginger in a gallon of water for approximately 10 minutes. Strain out spices and use the spicy water to brew a gallon of black tea. In a large saucepan combine the tea, the roasted oranges, one bottle of port (or red) wine, and sugar or honey to taste. Serve hot.

MAKES ABOUT 20 CUPS

FEBRUARY
Valentine Tea for Two

The month of February, otherwise unnoteworthy, has two things going for it: cold weather, which makes enjoying a warm fire even nicer, and the sweet celebration of St. Valentine's Day. For a very special evening, combine those two: a Valentine's Tea served in front of the fireplace.

If you have no fireplace, turn off the lights and fill the room with candles instead. Put some on windowsills so the flame is reflected in the glass, or on a flat mirror for double images.

Start your evening with champagne; end with hot tea laced with a fruity liqueur like Framboise or Cointreau. In between, serve a finger-food supper of small, elegant canapes, sweetheart sandwiches, and rich chocolate truffles from the candy shop.

If you're feeling really decadent, skip the supper and just have tea and dessert: chocolate fondue — a rich fudge sauce into which you dip pieces of fruit, biscotti, squares of pound cake, cookies, or your fingers. Worry about a balanced meal tomorrow.

Champagne

Sweetheart Sandwiches *

Cherry Oysters *

Caviar Puffs *

Passion Fruit Tarts *

Chocolate Truffles

Tea with Liqueur

If a small bit of loose tea floats to the top of your cup, you will soon be visited by an intriguing stranger.

Caviar Puffs

Make half of the recipe for small Pastry Puffs (page 32) and slice off the top of each. Mix ½ cup sour cream with 1 tablespoon lemon juice and fill each puff with about 1 teaspoonful of mixture. Top each with a dab of caviar.

10 SMALL PUFFS

Cherry Oysters

Drain 1 can of smoked oysters and blot off excess oil with paper towels. Toss the oysters in ¼ cup vinegar, preferably herb-flavored; drain well. Wash a pint of cherry tomatoes and cut a large X in the rounded end of each. Fit one oyster down into each X. Arrange tomatoes on a small tray or platter; garnish with lemon wedges or twists.

Sweeetheart Sandwiches

Cut sandwiches with a heart-shaped cookie cutter. Two suggestions: sliced turkey with cranberry mustard (mix Dijon mustard with whole cranberry sauce) on sourdough bread; or thin-sliced ham and Swiss cheese with herbed mayonnaise on pumpernickel.

"Love
and scandal are the best sweeteners of tea."
— Henry Fielding

Passion Fruit Tarts

First make tart shells: Roll out your favorite piecrust about ¼ inch thick (or thinner). Cut circles 1 inch wider than your muffin tins, and fit them into the bottoms of the muffin tins and partway up the sides. Prick bottoms with a fork. Bake at 350°F until lightly brown, about 10 minutes.

When cool, fill each to the top with fresh fruit: strawberries, kiwis, bananas, or some of each. To make a glaze, in a small saucepan mix ½ cup of cold passion fruit juice with 1 tablespoon cornstarch and simmer over medium heat until juice is clear and thickened. Spoon over fruit and refrigerate until glaze sets, at least 1 hour. (If you can't find passion fruit juice — so appropriate for the occasion! — substitute apple juice.) Melted currant jelly also makes a very pretty glaze.

½ CUP GLAZE (ENOUGH FOR SIX 3-INCH TARTS)

Liqueurs to Flavor Hot Tea

Grand Marnier, orange;
Amaretto, almond;
Crème de Mênthe, mint;
Framboise, raspberry;
Cherry Heering, cherry;
Calvados, apple;
Frangelico, hazelnut.

A splash of any fruit-flavored liqueur in your favorite hot tea makes a luscious treat.

MARCH
Breakfast in Bed

$\mathcal{A}$ little self-indulgence now and then is good for you. Breakfast in bed, alone or with your sweetie, is one of the best defenses against March's drab personality. Bring the tray and the Sunday paper, put on your favorite music, and unplug the telephone.

The whole idea is to spend time in bed, not in the kitchen. For that reason, the menu suggested here features do-ahead foods. To make it easier still, skip the eggs and serve yogurt with the fruit.

On the other hand, if you fancy something more substantial, plan items that are easy to eat in bed (no knife-and-fork action). For instance, home-fried potatoes made with bacon, onions, and green chilies; eggs baked in individual ramekins with mushroom or tomato sauce; roast beef hash with poached egg; quiche of your choice; hot fruit cobbler with flavored yogurt or whipped cream.

Creamy Scrambled Eggs ⁎

Bran Muffins ⁎

Honey-Orange Butter ⁎

Raspberry Jam

Fresh Fruit

Irish Breakfast Tea

Bran Muffins

This recipe makes a lot, but the batter will keep in the refrigerator for six weeks, so you can make just enough for one meal at a time. For a raisin or nut variation, add 2 cups raisins, 2 cups coarsely chopped nuts, or both to the batter.

2 cups whole-bran cereal (for example, All-Bran)	5 cups bran flakes (for example, Raisin Bran)
2 cups boiling water	1 cup vegetable oil
4½ cups flour	2 cups sugar
4½ teaspoons baking soda	4 eggs, beaten
2 teaspoons salt	1 quart buttermilk

Pour boiling water over whole-bran cereal and set aside. Sift flour, soda, and salt; add bran flakes; set aside. In a large bowl, mix oil and sugar. Stir beaten eggs into sugar mixture and gradually mix in buttermilk. Add the bran/water mixture, and then the flour/soda mixture. Stir until smooth. Fill muffin cups two-thirds full, and bake at 375°F for 20 to 25 minutes. Store remaining batter in covered jar in refrigerator; stir before using.

72 MUFFINS

Honey-Orange Butter

Soften ½ cup (1 stick) of butter or margarine. Stir in 2 tablespoons undiluted orange juice concentrate and 2 tablespoons honey; mix thoroughly. Make one day ahead, to let flavors blend.

MAKES ½ CUP

Making a Tea Cozy

To keep your tea hot while you dawdle, you can use one of those modern insulated containers designed for coffee, or do it the old-fashioned way: with a tea cozy. This thick fabric cover serves as a kind of blanket for the teapot, keeping your tea warm until you're ready to pour a second cup. Choose quilted fabric with a pretty print; ½ yard often makes two cozies. It's truly a simple stitchery project.

Measure your teapot and make a pattern out of paper; check for fit. Cut and stitch, following the sketches shown here.

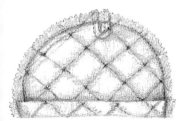 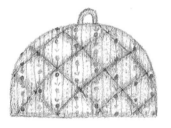

To make your cozy extra special, draw the outline of a teapot with washable marker and go over it with embroidery or fabric paint.

Creamy Scrambled Eggs

Beat together 4 eggs, 4 tablespoons half-and-half, and salt and pepper. You can do this part the night before; store in refrigerator in covered container. Come morning, stir in 1 tablespoon fresh herbs (your choice) and cook the eggs in 1 tablespoon butter until softly done. Transfer to small covered casserole dish, which you have preheated with hot water, and, if you wish, sprinkle with finely grated cheese — pepper Jack, shredded Parmesan, or smoked cheddar.
SERVES 2

APRIL

Easter Brunch

We are accustomed to thinking of coffee as the beverage of choice for brunch, but there's no reason it can't be tea. In fact, tea, with its warm but lighter taste, is perfect for the sunny/crisp days of April.

A cheerful and seasonal centerpiece for Easter Sunday brunch is a large glass bowl filled with colored eggs, either the traditional bright colors we all remember from childhood, or the softer tones of dyes you make from natural materials. After the meal (or before, if they can't wait that long), hide those same eggs for a children's egg hunt.

Earl Grey tea, with its soft undertone of orange, goes nicely with this menu. If the weather is warm enough, you may want to offer both hot and iced teas. In that case, make iced Earl Grey and offer guests a selection of teabags for hot tea.

*Fuzzy Navels** *and/or Orange Juice*

*Tea Sandwiches**

*Scotch Eggs**

Hot Cross Buns with Jam & Butter

*Banbury Tarts**

Carrot Cake

Earl Grey Tea

Earl Grey tea is named for a 19th-century Englishman who served as diplomat to China, where he learned to enjoy the orange-scented tea blend that still bears his name.

Homemade Natural Dyes for Eggs

Colorful vegetable material, spices, and tea itself all make excellent dyes. To create the dye-baths, dissolve the spices in hot water (1 to 2 tablespoons to 1 cup water); make a strong batch of tea; or simmer vegetable parts in just enough water to cover until the color is extracted, then strain.

Banbury Tarts

Raisins are traditional, but you could also make this with dried cranberries, in which case you'd have Cranberry Banbury Tarts.

1 cup raisins
1 cup sugar
1 egg, beaten
1 tablespoon melted butter
3 tablespoons fine cracker or bread crumbs
juice and grated rind of 1 lemon
pastry for a 1-crust pie

Mix filling ingredients together. Roll out pastry about ⅛ inch thick and cut into 3-inch squares. Place 1 scant tablespoon filling in the center and fold in half to make triangles; seal edges with water and cut a small X in the top. Bake at 350°F for 20 minutes, or until browned. You can use puff pastry instead of pie crust; bake at 400°F about 15 minutes.

MAKES 8 TO 10 TARTS

Fuzzy Navels

This delicious brunch cocktail made of orange juice (that's the "navel" part) and peach brandy (the "fuzz") tastes like springtime. Mix 1 part brandy with 6 to 8 parts juice. Have plain juice available, of course, for the children and any adults who prefer it.

Tea Sandwiches

Salmon and Dill. Spread the buttered bread with softened cream cheese, which you have thinned with a little cream and flavored with fresh (or dried) dill weed. Add an ultra-thin slice of smoked salmon or lox. Garnish with fresh dill, if available, or parsley sprig.

Curried Egg Salad. This is a good use of any eggs that got broken during your egg-coloring session. Chop 4 hard-cooked eggs, mix in ¼ cup mayonnaise (or half mayo and half plain yogurt) and 1½ teaspoons curry powder. Garnish with round slices of black or green olives.

Scotch Eggs

Start with peeled, hard-cooked eggs and any kind of bulk sausage you like; use about ¼ pound of sausage per egg. Divide your sausage and roll into large balls and then flatten to an oval about 5 inches long. Wrap each egg completely in sausage; dip your fingers in water and smooth together the seam and any cracks. You can do this much the day before; cover the pan with plastic wrap and refrigerate until party time. Bake at 400°F for about 30 minutes, until sausage is well done.

Natural Egg Dyes

❖ **Yellow onion skins** produce a dark yellow dye (In seconds an egg becomes golden yellow; left in longer, it turns the color of copper.)
❖ **Beets** make pastel pink
❖ **Blueberries** make blue-gray
❖ **Dried hibiscus flowers** (from herb shops and natural foods stores) produce lavender
❖ **Curry powder** makes a pale buttery yellow
❖ **Turmeric** makes golden yellow
❖ **Tea** produces a mellow terra-cotta brown

MAY
Mother's Day

$\mathcal{C}$elebrate the fullness of spring, and honor the mothers in your life, with a Sunday afternoon tea. A classic celebration would place your mother as guest of honor, surrounded by all her family with everyone making a glorious fuss over her. If your family geography permits that sort of gathering, you already know how lucky you are. If not, you can still celebrate the spirit of the holiday in other ways.

You might, for instance, host a "Great Mothers Tea." Invite friends (both men and women) who cannot for whatever reason spend the day with their own mothers. Ask them to choose a woman they admire and make her honorary mother-for-the-day. Over tea, encourage guests to introduce their "mother" by telling a bit about her. She doesn't have to be famous, or currently alive. She doesn't even have to be real; fictional characters have served many people as role models. The idea is to acknowledge women who have contributed something of value to humankind, and drink a cup of tea in their names.

Tea Sandwiches*

Chicken Puffs*

Raisin Scones* with Lemon Curd (page 45)

Fruit Cobbler

Apple-Mint Iced Tea*

Assorted Hot Teas

Apple-Mint Iced Tea

Mix 2 cups apple juice, 1 quart water, and 1 cup of chopped fresh mint leaves and bring to boil. Add 6 teaspoons of loose tea or 6 to 8 teabags, and steep 5 minutes. Strain and chill. Serve over ice with fresh mint leaves. Makes 1½ quarts.

Pastry Puffs

You can make these little puffs either savory or sweet. For dessert puffs, add 2 tablespoons sugar to the flour.

½ cup water
¼ cup butter
½ cup flour

2 eggs, room temperature
2 tablespoons sugar (optional)
pinch of salt

Combine water and butter in a saucepan, and boil until butter is melted. Remove from heat. Add flour, optional sugar, and a pinch of salt all at once and stir quickly until mixture is smooth and forms a thick ball. Thoroughly beat in eggs, one at a time. Place spoonfuls of dough on greased cookie sheets: 1 teaspoonful 1 inch apart for very small puffs, or 1 tablespoonful 2 inches apart for larger puffs. Bake at 400°F for 10 minutes, then 350°F for 10 minutes more, until golden brown and crisp.
MAKES 25 TO 30 MIDGET-SIZED PUFFS OR TEN 2-INCH PUFFS

Chicken Puffs

Make chicken salad your favorite way and refrigerate. Make pastry puffs, using recipe above. Slice off the top one-third, fill with a spoonful of chicken salad, and cover with the pastry top. You can make the puffs a day or so ahead and then keep them in an airtight container.

Tea Sandwiches

Cheese-Nut. Beat a large brick of cream cheese until smooth. Thin with about ¼ cup milk, and divide into two equal portions. To one half, mix in ½ cup diced celery and ½ cup chopped walnuts. Spread on whole wheat bread.

Fruit and Cheese. To the remaining cream cheese, mix in 1 cup finely chopped pineapple bits, very well drained. Spread on pumpernickel or Boston brown bread.

Raisin Scones

To the Basic Scones recipe on page 48, add 3 tablespoons sugar and ½ cup raisins. Serve with Lemon Curd (page 45).

The Language of Flowers

The time is right, and the occasion is perfect, to indulge yourself with a houseful of spring flowers. With just a little knowledge of the centuries-old symbolism attached to flowers and herbs, you can create a Mother's Day bouquet that sends a silent, fragrant message of love and appreciation.

Agrimony for thankfulness

Angelica for inspiration

Borage for courage

White carnation for devotion

Chamomile for patience

Lilac for a baby's first love

Pansy for "thinking of you"

Rose for love

Rosemary for remembrance

Sage for wisdom

Tulips for love

JUNE

Bridal Shower

*O*rchestrating a wedding is a harrowing task. With this afternoon tea, you can offer the bride-to-be something she sorely needs: an hour or two of sweet calm.

Strive for a tranquil atmosphere. Minimize your own scurrying by setting the table and preparing all foods ahead of time. Play quiet, soothing music in the background. Have one pot of tea at the ready when the first guests arrive.

This is a tea party shower in more ways than one: the gift theme is items to outfit the bride for her own tea parties. If guests need ideas, some ideal suggestions might be sugar tongs, Victorian-style strainers, tea balls in several sizes, unusual teas she may not have tried before, dainty napkins, or teapots plain or fancy. Most fun of all, pretty cup-and-saucer sets — the guests will have the fun of browsing in secondhand or antique shops, and the bride will have an instant collection.

For an easy and beautiful cake for this occasion, order one from the bakery, using the bride's favorite colors. Tell the baker to allow room on the finished cake for fresh flowers. At home, transfer the cake to a large cake plate and surround it with edible flowers, including some on the cake itself. Be sure to use flowers that you know have not been sprayed, which means homegrown.

Tea Sandwiches *

Maids of Honor *

Meringue Kisses *

Chocolate-Dipped Strawberries *

Bride's Cake

Iced Lemon Spice Tea

Hot Tea

Favorite edible *flowers include nasturtiums, pansies, calendulas, roses, carnations, and any herb flowers, especially chives, lavender, borage, and bergamot.*

Chocolate-Dipped Strawberries

Select large berries with stems attached. Wash gently and air-dry thoroughly. Melt 1 cup chocolate chips with 1 teaspoon of vegetable shortening in top of double boiler. Dip bottom half of berry into chocolate, and lay on wax-paper-lined cookie sheets until chocolate cools and sets.

Maids of Honor

These almond tarts, first baked at the court of Henry VIII and named for the queen's ladies-in-waiting, are served here in honor of the bride's attendants. They are very sweet; you may want to serve them with a dollop of unsweetened whipped cream.

Butter the insides of muffin tins and sprinkle on flour, shaking off excess. Roll out your favorite piecrust (or a purchased crust) and cut circles that are about 1 inch wider than the muffin cups. Fit dough into the muffin cups and partway up the sides.

Beat together 2 egg yolks, ½ cup sugar, ½ cup ground almonds, 1 tablespoon grated lemon zest, and 1 tablespoon flour. Slowly add 2 tablespoons cream, and beat until mixture is smooth. Add about 1 tablespoon filling to each pastry cup (should not reach the top). Bake at 350°F for 15 to 20 minutes, until filling is golden brown.

Meringue Kisses

Mix together 1 cup sugar, 2 teaspoons cinnamon, and a pinch of salt. Beat 2 egg whites until slightly stiff; add in sugar mixture a bit at a time while continuing to beat. When egg whites are stiff, mix in any of the following: about 1 cup chocolate bits, chopped nuts, flaked coconut, raisins or currants; ⅛ cup grated orange or lemon peel; a few drops of mint or almond extract; a few drops of vanilla, or ⅛ cup crystallized ginger chopped very fine. Drop spoonfuls onto well-greased cookie sheets and bake on middle rack at 325°F for about 20 minutes.

Tussy-Mussy for the Bride

This pretty nosegay has one flat side, so that it will lie gracefully on the table or the bride's plate as a place marker. Cut your flowers and herbs the morning of the party. After making the tussy-mussy, mist it with water and store it in a plastic bag in the refrigerator.

If you have rosemary growing in your garden, snip two or three short pieces for each guest, tie them together with a ribbon; and attach to each placecard. Inscribe the guest's name and the message, "Here's rosemary for remembrance!"

Tea Sandwiches

For an attractive sandwich tray, use three different kinds of bread (such as sourdough, dark rye, and whole wheat).

Chicken Tarragon. Whip butter with chopped fresh or dried tarragon and a splash of lemon juice. Spread on bread a bit more thickly than usual. Add slices of chicken breast, and top with crumbled bacon.

Ham and Apricot. Mix 3 parts cream cheese with 1 part apricot preserves; blend well. Top with sliced ham.

Cheese-Nut. Make a cheese spread of grated cheddar and mayonnaise, in approximately equal parts. Mix in chopped pecans.

JULY

Tea & Roses

$\mathcal{A}$mong the many old-fashioned roses is the group known as "tea roses." First introduced into Europe in the mid-nineteenth century, they were given their name by some unknown person — an Englishman, no doubt — who thought they smelled like a newly opened tin of tea (perhaps because most tea imported to England in those days was perfumed with flowers).

For July, when most roses are still blooming their hearts out, plan an afternoon dessert tea built around this favorite garden beauty. The more roses, the better. If you don't have your own, collaborate with a gardening friend. Or volunteer an afternoon's work session in the rose beds at a church or a community garden in exchange for some of the flowers.

If you have a garden and friendly weather, set up your party table among the roses. If not, fill the indoors with the smell of roses by simmering a few drops of rose oil (available in herb, craft, and gift shops, and some natural food stores) in a small pot of water.

For the table, the main centerpiece is a huge arrangement of roses. Lightly scatter flower petals over the tabletop. Tie napkins into soft folds (see drawing on page 41) and slip a flower under the ribbon. If you have, or have access to, a cup-and-saucer collection, now is the time to use it.

Raspberry/Nut Scones with Raspberry Butter*

Cheesecake Squares*

Rose Sugar Cookies*

Brandy Snaps* with Whipped Cream

Honey-Roasted Nuts

Rosehip Tea

$\mathcal{T}eas$ made from rose hips, the cranberry-size red fruits that develop after flowers fade, are rich in vitamin C.

Tea & Roses 39

Brandy Snaps

6 tablespoons butter
¼ cup corn syrup
¼ cup brown sugar
½ cup flour
1 teaspoon ground ginger

⅛ teaspoon ground cardamom
1 teaspoon brandy
½ teaspoon grated lemon zest
(from one-half lemon)
whipped cream

In a small saucepan, heat butter, syrup, and sugar over low heat until butter melts. Remove from heat. Stir in flour and spices, mixing until smooth. Stir in brandy and lemon zest. Drop teaspoonfuls of batter 4 inches apart on well-greased baking sheet. Bake in preheated 350°F oven 5 to 7 minutes, until cookies are lacy and browned. Meanwhile, butter the handles of several wooden spoons. Let cookies cool very briefly (10 seconds or so), then, one at a time, lift off with a wide spatula and wrap around a spoon handle. Cool completely, then twist off. Work as fast as you can; if cookies become too stiff to roll, return them to warm oven for a few minutes. Traditionally, the cylinders are filled with a squirt of whipped cream.

MAKES ABOUT 20 COOKIES

Raspberry/Nut Scones

To the Basic Scones recipe (page 48), carefully fold in 1 cup fresh or frozen raspberries and ½ cup chopped nuts. Blend raspberry jam into softened butter for a spread.

For a natural skin freshener, add a handful of rose petals (which are mildly astringent) to a pot of steeping black tea. Strain after 15 minutes; store in refrigerator.

Victorian Napkins

Start with a large square napkin; fold in half and then half again. Pleat into accordion folds about 1 inch wide. Tie the middle with a pretty ribbon, and the top and bottom will automatically fan out. Slip a rosebud or a sprig of dried lavender under the bow.

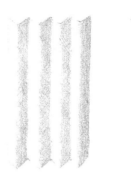

Rose Sugar Cookies

Frost storebought or homemade sugar cookies with icing that has the color, flavor, and look of a rose. Make icing from 1 cup confectioner's sugar and 2 tablespoons milk; add a few drops of rosewater flavoring (available at gourmet food shops). Using red food coloring, tint two-thirds of the icing light pink and one-third a darker pink. Cover each cookie with the light pink icing; refrigerate until icing is firm. Using a pastry bag fitted with a very narrow tip (or readymade icing-in-a-tube), pipe several concentric circles of the darker icing on each cookie; the circles should be close to each other but not touching. With the blade of a table knife, start at the outermost circle and drag a line through the dark icing to the middle of the cookie; repeat all around. Now, instead of circles you have scallops representing the petals of a stylized rose.

Cheesecake Squares

Use your favorite cheesecake recipe. Press a crumb crust into a square cake pan; fill with cheesecake filling and bake. When cool, cut into squares.

AUGUST
The Queen's Tea

Among the British people, no member of the Royal Family is more beloved than the "Queen Mum," the mother of Queen Elizabeth and grandmother of those news-making princes. Born daughter of a Scottish earl in 1900, she married the man who eventually became His Majesty King George VI, and she reigned as Queen of England from 1936 to 1952. In honor of her birthday, August 4, for this month we plan an elegant tea party featuring all things British. And let's present it in the traditional sequence: After the tea is poured, first the sandwiches and other savories are served, then scones with Devon cream (see page 12), and finally the sweets.

What's in a Name?

When someone says "high tea," do you picture an elegant affair with dainty cucumber sandwiches and tiny sweet cakes? High tea is actually a supper; it is served around six o'clock, and everyone sits at table. High tea features hearty, filling foods, including at least one hot dish such as shepherd's pie or Welsh rabbit. The other tea, the one with the cucumber sandwiches, is called afternoon tea. A great many Americans get the terminology wrong (and a great deal more, some British say).

*Tea Sandwiches**
*Curry Puffs**
Scones (page 48)
*Lemon Curd Tarts**
Assam or Ceylon Tea

The British drink an average of six cups of tea per day per person.

Singing Hinny and More

There are many kinds of British tea cakes, some with wonderful names: "singing hinny" (a sconelike griddle cake that sizzles as it cooks); "fat rascal" (plump scone studded with raisins); "small-coal fizzer" (a version of singing hinny from coal mining country); "lardy cake" (a butter-rich bun once made with lard); and "petticoat tails" (a shortbread cookie).

Tea Sandwiches

Three classic and very British tea sandwiches are cucumber, egg and watercress, and radish.

Cucumber. Slice cucumber as thinly as possible; lay in a colander and sprinkle with vinegar and salt; let drain about 30 minutes. Spread white bread with softened butter, cover thoroughly with several layers of cucumbers, then second slice of bread. Trim off crusts; cut into triangles.

Egg and Watercress. Butter slices of rye bread; cover with watercress, then overlapping slices of hard-cooked egg; top with second piece of buttered bread. Trim crusts, and cut into fingers.

Radish. Butter slices of a dark bread such as pumpernickel, and cut into fourths. Cover with overlapping slices of radish; leave open-face.

Curry Puffs

First thaw a sheet of frozen puff pastry (see page 60), then make Curry Cream Sauce: In saucepan, melt 1 tablespoon butter; add 1 tablespoon flour and 1 teaspoon curry powder and stir well. Cook over low heat 2 or 3 minutes, then remove from heat. Gradually stir in ½ cup milk, mixing until smooth. Return to heat and cook until thick. Remove from heat. Mix in 4 ounces of chopped shrimp, and salt and pepper to taste; set aside. Cut small circles from puff pastry; sandwich a spoonful of shrimp mixture between two circles. Moisten the edges and crimp them together with a fork. Place on greased baking sheet, paint with beaten egg, and bake at 450°F 10 to 15 minutes, until puffed and brown.

Lemon Curd

4 eggs
2 cups sugar
⅛ teaspoon salt
¼ cup butter

½ cup lemon juice
2 tablespoons grated lemon
  zest

Beat together eggs, sugar, and salt. Stir in butter, lemon juice, and lemon zest. Cook in double boiler until thick, about 30 minutes, stirring frequently. Cool to room temperature; store in refrigerator. Curd is thicker when cold.

MAKES ABOUT 1½ CUPS

Lemon Curd Tarts

Make baked tart shells using piecrust pastry in muffin pans or individual tart pans (page 21). When cool, fill with lemon curd. If you wish, add fresh berries on top.

Rosy Sugar

Sugar flavored with the seductive fragrance of roses is doubly sweet; it makes an ordinary cup of tea something extra-ordinary. Layer petals from *unsprayed* roses with sugar in a jar that closes tightly; after a few weeks, sift out the petals. Store sugar in a covered container.

*J*ust as we're coming to terms with the inevitable approach of cold winter weather, September often offers us a surprise: the blue sky and soft warm air of Indian Summer. It's a perfect time for a hike to your family's favorite picnic spot.

Fill your backpack with foods that travel well, meaning they don't require constant refrigeration and are sturdy enough to withstand a few bumps along the way. Bring along iced tea, because hiking makes you hot and thirsty, and also hot tea (in a thermos), because you may feel cool when you stop moving for any length of time.

For iced tea on the trail, make your tea the day before and freeze in a plastic drink container overnight; it will defrost in your pack while you hike. *Hiker's trick:* Wrap a washcloth around the frozen jug to catch the condensation; use the damp cloth to refresh your face and hands.

Make the ginger/fennel base for the hot tea by simmering 4 or 5 slices of fresh ginger and about 1 tablespoon of fennel seeds in water. (If you don't like the taste of licorice, skip the fennel.) When it is very fragrant, strain out the spices. Bring the flavored water to a boil and use that to brew your tea; use a strong blend like Irish Breakfast so the ginger doesn't overpower the taste of the tea.

*Scones, Butter, & Jam**

*Cornish Pasties**

*"Gorp" Cookies**

Carrot & Celery Sticks

Pickled Green Beans

*Hot Ginger/Fennel Tea**

Iced Tea

*W*hen covered with boiling water, the dried, twisted leaves of loose tea slowly unfurl — a process known as "the agony of the leaves."

A Nice Cuppa

All of Great Britain
comes to a standstill at
4:00, while someone
puts the kettle on for a
"cuppa." The British
even carry a small
camper's stove and a
kettle when they vaca-
tion in Europe, and stop
by the side of the road
for their "brew-up."

Basic Scones

*There are scores of scone variations (see page 12). For slight
sweetness, add ¼ cup sugar. For richness, use cream instead of the
milk. You can also add 1 egg (decrease milk to ½ cup) or increase
the amount of butter for richer texture.*

2 cups flour	4 tablespoons butter
2½ teaspoons baking powder	¾ cup milk
¼ teaspoon salt	

Sift dry ingredients. Cut in butter until crumbly (a food proces-
sor helps here). Add milk and blend well; dough will be sticky.
Flour a flat workspace and knead the dough for about half a
minute. Roll out ½ inch thick and cut into whatever shape you
like (triangles are traditional). Bake at 400°F for about 15 minutes.
MAKES ABOUT 12 SCONES, DEPENDING ON SIZE

"Gorp" Cookies

Gorp is the backpackers' name for that free-for-all mixture of
peanuts, raisins, seeds, candies, and what-have-you that is sometimes known as *trail mix.* To make Gorp Cookies, start with a
basic recipe for oatmeal-raisin cookies; add to the dough any or
all of these: sunflower seeds, M&Ms, chopped nuts, dried
coconut strips, chopped dates, chocolate chips, and peanut
butter or butterscotch bits. The more stuff you include, the gor-
pier the cookies.

Cornish Pasties

A traditional British version is given here, but in fact these turnovers are very flexible: the filling can be any combination of meats and vegetables, including all kinds of leftovers.

For the filling, trim all fat from ½ pound of chuck steak and chop the steak finely. Peel and chop 1 large potato and 1 large onion. Mix together with salt and pepper to taste. Roll out piecrust for a one-crust pie and cut into 3-inch circles. Place a large spoonful of meat mixture on each circle and fold in half; seal edges with water and prick vent holes in tops. Bake at 400°F for 10 minutes, then 40 minutes at 325°F. (If you're using leftover meat that's already cooked, you need only about 20 minutes total.)

MAKES 10 TO 12

Variation: Instead of Cornish Pasties, you may wish to take along other filled pastries like empenadas or calzones. Or, choose Southern-style ham biscuits: Bake biscuits and slit open like a sandwich. Cut thick slices of ham into squares the approximate size of the biscuits. Fry ham slices and put them directly into the biscuit, letting the biscuit catch the ham juices.

Fennel is reputed to boost energy. Roman soldiers nibbled the seeds all day long to stave off hunger on long marches; so did the Egyptian slaves who built the pyramids.

On any special occasion, make a child feel even more special with a tea party in her or his honor. For birthdays, to celebrate an achievement, or for no reason except the fun of it, invite some of the child's friends for an afternoon tea. It's a nice activity for October, when the weather argues for indoor pleasures.

Children love ceremony. Did you ever watch a toddler hosting a pretend tea party, carefully pouring invisible tea into toy cups? In a few years that same child will be old enough to serve the real thing and will do it with the same sense of enchantment.

You and the young host can prepare and arrange the party food ahead of time, but when the guests arrive let the host be in charge as much as possible. (Decide, based on age, whether the child needs help serving hot tea.)

Finger Sandwiches

Orange Gelatin Wedges *

Peanut Butter/Celery Rounds *

Jam Tarts *

Mock Ice Cream Cupcakes *

Hot Tea & Lemonade

An old superstition holds that if two women pour tea from the same pot, one of them will give birth to a redheaded child within a year.

Handmade Invitations

Have the child who is hosting the party make a drawing of a teapot or teacup. On the same piece of paper (make a photo-reduction if necessary), the adult-in-charge will write in the specifics — date, time, and any special dress. Make photocopies on white or colored paper, and have the child color and sign each one. Roll up like parchment and tie with a pretty ribbon; hand deliver.

Peanut Butter/Celery Rounds

For this elegant variation on an old favorite, fill three (or six) celery stalks very full with peanut butter, mounding smoothly at the top. (This is easier if the peanut butter is at room temperature.) Press three filled celery stalks together, peanut butter side facing inward, until the edges of the celery touch each other; wipe away any excess peanut butter that squeezes through. Wrap tightly in waxed paper or plastic wrap, and refrigerate for at least an hour. To serve, cut the celery logs into half-inch slices; you'll have scalloped circles of celery with peanut butter centers.

Finger Sandwiches

Let the young host or hostess decide what kind of sandwiches the guests will like and cut them into "fingers" or other small shapes.

Mock Ice Cream Cupcakes

Purchase ice cream cones that have flat bottoms, so that you can stand them upright in muffin tins. Make a batch of your favorite cupcake mix. Fill the cones with the mix, up to ½ inch below the rim. Bake as usual. The baked cakes will puff up above the rim, in a shape like ice cream piled in a cone. Frost the top and cover with small candies or sprinkles.

Orange Gelatin Wedges

Cut oranges in half from top to bottom (not through their equators). Using your fingers and a small spoon, remove all the orange pulp; set aside for another use. Leave all the white pith and make sure no holes appear. Place the empty orange shells in muffin tins, for stability. Choose a favorite flavor of gelatin with an eye to color as well as taste: what looks good with orange? Make according to package directions, except use ¼ cup less water. Fill the orange cups completely to the rim; refrigerate until set. To serve, remove orange cups from muffin tin. Slice each lengthwise into two or three crescents. Plan on one-half orange per child; one 3-ounce package of gelatin fills 4 large orange cups (2 oranges).

Jam Tarts

Make or buy miniature tart shells. Fill with a thin layer of fruit preserves or jam; top with whipped cream.

Children's Tea Sets

The miniature tea sets we now think of as gifts for children were originally created in the late nineteenth century by china manufacturers as salesmen's samples. But when salesmen made their presentation to homemakers, the mothers wanted to buy the tiny sets for their children.

Party for a Shut-In

One of the nicest things you can do for a friend who is homebound is to pack up a portable tea party and take it over. Set up the tea table beside the bed, if your friend is confined to bed; or near a window if he or she is able to move to a chair.

Come prepared with happy things to show, share, and talk about. Be on the lookout for interesting and funny stories in the local newspaper. Bring recent pictures of family members or mutual friends. Encourage your children to draw a get-well or thinking-of-you picture. If it seems appropriate, bring the children along; it's a good experience for them and surely a treat for the shut-in.

If your friend must stay in bed, think about the "crumbliness" factor when you plan your menu. Finger-foods may be easiest. It's probably simplest to boil the water and brew the tea once you arrive, but bring everything with you, including the teapot, unless you are sure you will be able to use your friend's without inconvenience.

For this kind of tea party, your "guest of honor" will appreciate finger towels. Bring along small towels, sliced lemons, a bowl, and a small tray. While you're having tea, keep water boiling in the kitchen. Near the end of the meal, slip out and pour boiling water over lemon slices in the bowl. Push the towels down into the water to cover them. When cool enough to handle, wring out towels, roll them up, and bring them in on the tray.

Tea Sandwiches *

Savory Bites *

Skewered Fruit *

Cake Fingers with Fruit Sauce *

Herb Tea

A special treat for someone who's feeling "blah": sweeten herbal tea with fruit preserves.

Teas That Heal

The medicinal value of certain herbs is well established; tea brewed from them is healing as well as soothing. Some traditional favorite teas for colds and sore throats are horehound, mint, lemon balm, and sage. For nausea or cramps, peppermint. For digestive calm, anise, fennel, and lemon verbena.

Savory Bites

½ pound mushrooms, sliced
2 tablespoons butter
4 eggs, beaten
1 cup sour cream
1 cup cottage cheese
½ cup grated Parmesan cheese
4 tablespoons flour
¼ teaspoon salt
2 cups shredded cheese (cheddar, Swiss, or Montery Jack or a combination)

Sauté the mushrooms in the butter, drain, and set aside. Blend eggs, sour cream, cottage and Parmesan cheeses, flour, and salt in a large bowl. Mix in mushrooms and cheese. (At this point you can add other optional ingredients such as shrimp, crab, ham, bacon, broccoli, etc.) Pour into greased 10-inch pie pan and bake at 350°F about 45 minutes. Serve this crustless quiche at room temperature, cut into wedges for table seating, or bite-size squares for eating in bed.

MAKES 6 TO 8 WEDGES OR ABOUT FIFTY 1-INCH SQUARES

Cake Fingers with Fruit Sauce

Use a firm-textured, noncrumbly cake such as a dense pound cake or fruitcake. Cut into slices ½ inch thick, then fingers 1 inch wide. Use a blender to puree fresh or frozen raspberries, strawberries, peaches, or another favorite fruit. Simmer fruit until slightly thick, and sweeten with sugar, to taste. For individual servings at the table, pour over cake slices; to serve as finger-food, place puree in a small cup and use as a dipping sauce.

Skewered Fruit

Cut fresh or canned fruit into small one-bite cubes, and insert a toothpick in each. For table seating, you can substitute a mixed fruit compote.

Tea Sandwiches

Use white or whole wheat bread, and fillings that are familiar, rather than exotic. *Suggestions:* Egg salad, deviled ham, salmon spread, cream cheese blended with orange marmalade. Closed sandwiches, cut into small pieces or fingers, are easier to eat in bed than open-face ones.

DECEMBER

Holiday Open House

tea party open house is a refreshing change from the cocktail party atmosphere. And, because tea foods can be made ahead and served at room temperature, the logistics are easier. You can, if you prefer, plan a party entirely without alcohol. Or set up a "tea bar" of brandies and liqueurs in one corner, and invite guests to add a splash to their cup.

Continuously brewing pots of tea for a large gathering is impractical. Either set out a selection of teabags along with a large insulated carafe of hot water, or make up a tea concentrate ahead of time and dilute it with hot water that you keep simmering on the stove (see box, page 11). Have one carafe of brewed tea ready when the first guests arrive, then duck into the kitchen to refill it as needed.

To make your house smell wonderful for this occasion, simmer a mixture of mulling spices (cinnamon sticks, whole cloves, whole allspice, and dried lemon peel) on the stove for about an hour before the party.

Red and Green Sandwiches*

Cheese Straws

Sausage Rolls*

Mincemeat Turnovers*

Stuffed Apricots*

Fruit Tarts (page 21)

Fruitcake

Christmas Cookies

Wassail*

Selection of Teas

Red and Green Sandwiches

Prepare firm white bread and cut slices into 4 squares. On half the pieces, spread a layer of "green" mayonnaise (mayo plus lots of chopped parsley) or softened cream cheese mixed with pesto; top with crosswise slices of a small Roma-type tomato or half a cherry tomato. On the other pieces of bread, spread a mixture of cream cheese and tomato paste and top with slices of unpeeled English cucumber. Make sure some of the spread is visible around the topping. Arrange in a checkerboard pattern on a serving tray.

Sausage Rolls

Frozen puff pastry is available in supermarkets, usually two 11" x 14" sheets to a package. If you make a large batch of these rolls, thaw all the pastry but keep it cold and work with just one sheet at a time. You can also use piecrust pastry.

Thaw one sheet of frozen puff pastry and cut lengthwise in halves or thirds, depending on the size of your sausage. Lay a line of link sausages down each piece, fold pastry over sausages, and seal the edges with water. Cut crosswise into 2-inch sections, if sausage is fat, or between links for slender sausages. Place seam side down on greased baking sheet and brush with beaten egg. Bake at 450°F for 30 minutes. Refrigerate until the party; serve at room temperature.

Mincemeat Turnovers

You can use commercial mincemeat for this recipe, either a 9-ounce package or a 27-ounce jar. If you wish, embellish the mixture by adding chopped fresh apple or pear, nuts, or dried cranberries. For the turnovers, make or buy piecrust pastry, roll out ⅛ inch thick, and cut into 2½-inch rounds. Put a teaspoonful of mincemeat on each, fold over into a semicircle, and seal and crimp edges with tines of a fork. Bake at 350°F about 20 minutes. MAKES ABOUT 50

Wassail

You can substitute other juices or combinations of juices, such as pineapple, orange, or peach.

4 quarts water	4 sticks cinnamon
20 teabags or ½ cup black tea leaves	1 gallon apple juice or cider
1 cup sugar	1 quart cranberry juice
	½ cup lemon juice

Boil water; add tea, sugar, and cinnamon. Let steep for 5 minutes. Strain and add fruit juices. Chill and serve in punch bowl, or serve hot in a dispensing urn.

MAKES 36 CUPS

Make up small cheesecloth bags of your mulling spices, tie on an instruction card, and give one to each departing guest as a party favor.

Stuffed Apricots

For 1 pound of dried apricots, whip one 3-ounce package of softened cream cheese with 2 tablespoons plain or lemon-flavored yogurt or milk. Add lemon juice, confectioner's sugar to taste, and 1 tablespoon finely chopped nuts (optional). With a sharp knife slit open one side of each dried apricot and fold out like a butterfly. Fill with ½ to 1 teaspoon of the filling; press the cut edges back together. Refrigerate for an hour, or until cheese is firm. Melt ½ cup chocolate chips with ½ teaspoon vegetable shortening in double boiler or microwave and dip the apricots halfway. Place in a single layer on waxed paper until chocolate is set.

MAKES ABOUT 75

Bedtime Tea

Hot Tea Toddy

Here's a special treat for a cold winter's night: strong tea, plus a spoonful of your favorite warmer-upper: brandy, rum, Irish whiskey, or Bailey's Irish Cream.

This book contains ideas for tea parties, and parties, by definition, involve at least two people. Now, as your final tea event, you are permitted — nay, encouraged — to treat yourself to a quiet hour alone. Indulge yourself with all your favorite things: favorite kind of tea, favorite cookie or tea bread, favorite music, and favorite book, all in your favorite chair.

In the evening, you may prefer to avoid teas with caffeine. All herbal teas are caffeine-free, but some are especially nice at bedtime. Mint teas are restful and calming, especially if your tummy is feeling a bit queasy. After a heavy meal, try a blend with anise; it tastes like licorice and aids digestion.

Chamomile, perhaps the best-known of all herbal teas, is perfect for late evening. It has a gentle flavor and aroma, and it contains a natural, perfectly safe sedative that will help you fall asleep. For over two thousand years, people have enjoyed chamomile to bring a soft close to their stressful day.

Goodnight, sleepyhead — sweet dreams!

Index